M000022333

THINK

HOME

LOANS

Louis Schornstein (NMLS #5490)
888-999-1929
lschornstein@ptmcorp.net
275 Route 22 East
Springfield, NJ 07081
Equal Housing Lender

To the best of our knowledge, the information contained herein is accurate and reliable as of the date of publication; however, we do not assume any liability whatsoever for the accuracy and completeness of the below information.

Any information given in this book should not be mistaken for legal advice. It is the customers' responsibility to determine which mortgage program would suit your needs the best.

"Home is the nicest word there is."

- Laura Ingalls Wilder

To my beautiful family whose unwavering support and love continues to motivate me to be a better person and the best advocate for my clients.

Louis

Table of Contents

1. Different Types Of Homes | pg. 12

2. HOA Docs | pg. 16

3. Special Financing Programs | pg. 18

4. Be Prepared To Act Fast | pg. 21

5. Buyers Agents Cost | pg. 23

6. Pre-Approval | pg. 24

7. Home Buying Process | pg. 25

8. Keep an Open Mind | pg. 30

9. Agent You Like | pg. 32

10. Point of a Home Inspection | pg. 33

11. Leave Your Money Alone | pg. 35

12. Online vs Local People | pg. 37

13. Multiple Neighborhood Visits | pg. 39

14. Write a Love Letter | pg. 41

15. Auction Traps | pg. 42

16. When To Talk to a Loan Officer | pg. 43

17. Credit Scores | pg. 44

18. What We Look At | pg. 46

19. What is Pre-Approval | pg. 48

20. Minimum Down Payments | pg. 50

21. Cash You'll Need | pg. 51

22. Discount Points | pg. 52

23. When Discount Points Are Good | pg. 53

24. Fixed Rate vs ARM Loan | pg. 54

25. PITI | pg. 55

26. Gift Funds | pg. 56

27. Why Buy |pg. 57

28. How Much House | pg. 59

29. How Long Does It Take | pg. 60

30. Messed Up Credit Options | pg. 61

31. Earnest Money | pg. 62

32. Money For Repairs |pg. 63

33. What is an Appraisal | pg. 64

34. Home For You vs Investment Home |pg. 65

35. 4 Questions For Flips | pg. 67

36. Condos | pg. 70

37. What Are Contingencies | pg. 73

38. Down Payment Options | pg. 76

39. Let's Talk About Sewers | pg. 79

40. 5 Reasons To Use VA Loans | pg. 81

41. 15 Year vs 30 Year Mortgage | pg. 85

42. More Money Down | pg. 88

43. Do You Like To Gamble | pg. 91

44. 10 Commandments of Home Buyers | pg. 96

45. Prepare Early | pg. 100

Conclusion | pg. 104

1. Know The Difference Between Different Types Of Homes You Can Purchase

When you're a first time homebuyer and you're going out looking at purchasing your first place and escaping the apartment life, it's helpful to know the different types of properties that exist.

There are four main types of properties.

Each one has positives and negatives and we're going to go over the different types of homes you can purchase.

Single Family Home

The first is a single family home. This is the most common type of home purchased. It's what you're used to seeing in a neighborhood where it's a detached home usually with a garage and there's going to be space in between each house.

This is the most common type of home purchase in America.

It's the kind of place that people will purchase when they think about the American Dream but it is not the only type of property.

There are other types of homes that work for different types of people as well.

Condos

The second kind of property is a Condo. A Condo is similar to an apartment but everybody in the complex owns their unit.

In a condo you own everything inside your walls. Everything outside your walls is either common space, owned by somebody else, or belongs to the complex itself.

When you own a condo, you're going to have a condominium association fee every month or every year.

These fees will cover things like your amenities, taking care of the parking lots, security, and things like that.

Condos are great for people who want to be in a close environment but have the security of ownership.

Townhomes

The third type of property that's available is a townhome.

A townhome is similar to a condo in that you have shared walls, but with a townhome you own everything inside of your unit as well as the front and back of it.

You typically have some property with a townhome.

Most townhomes are going to be two stories with a small front yard and a small backyard.

Occasionally, you will see townhome complexes that also have garages.

Duplex

The fourth type of property is a duplex.

A duplex is a unit that has two homes attached in the middle.

Typically if you own a duplex, you're going to own the entire unit. In some areas you may be able to buy only one half of the duplex.

You would own everything inside your unit as well as your yard with one shared wall with your neighbor.

2. Ask To See Any Homeowners Association Documents Before You Make an Offer or During Your Inspection Period

It's really important to know what's required before you buy into a neighborhood. Every homeowners association or HOA is a little bit different in what they allow and what they don't allow.

They also have different requirements of the homeowners and different association dues and you want to know all of these things before you move into a neighborhood.

Let's say for example you own a motorhome and it's important to you to be able to park that at your house. You want to read the HOA documents to make sure that's an option.

Some neighborhoods don't allow motorhomes and you have to put it in storage. So that's one example of why it's important to get all the Homeowner's Association documents before you make an offer.

If that's not possible you can review the documents during your inspection period. You will have the ability to get out of the contract during the inspection period if you find something in the HOA docs you don't like.

3. Find Out If You Qualify For Any Special Financing Programs

One of the reasons it's important to talk with a lender before you start going out looking at houses is so you can know exactly which mortgage programs you qualify for and how much home you can afford based on the payment you want.

There are some special programs and government programs that make it easier for renters to become homeowners or for people to move up into new homes.

The **VA Loan Program** is one example.

VA stands for Veterans Administration and this is a loan that is available for most veterans and active duty military.

There are some requirements, so you'll want to speak with a Loan Officer to make sure that you do qualify. They can also help you get the Certificate of Eligibility from the VA showing that you qualify.

The VA loan is really great because it doesn't require a downpayment. It actually covers 100% of your loan amount.

In most cases, it will save you several thousand dollars out-of-pocket since you can keep the down payment.

Another type of special program is the **FHA Program**.

This was designed for first time homebuyers to be able to bring only a small down payment at closing.

In most cases, the FHA program only requires a 3.5% down payment compared to a normal conventional home loan that requires a 10 or 20% down payment.

You can see how much you can save using the FHA program.

The third government program that helps home buyers get into a house with little or no money out of pocket is the **USDA Program**.

This was designed for rural communities and typically is available in more country areas.

This program is great for those homebuyers because it also does not require a downpayment and provides 100% financing.

There also maybe some **local grants** available that you qualify for.

In some cases, those grants will cover your down payment or parts of your closing costs or may even cover both of those things.

You'll want to speak with a local professional to find out if you qualify for any grant programs that currently exist.

These programs can change pretty quickly because sometimes the money is limited and will run out fast.

So, if you find out you qualify for a grant program you should move quickly while the money is still available.

4. Be Prepared To Act Fast When You Find What You Want

What that means is not to delay putting an offer on a home when it meets your needs and you feel like it's the one for you.

Depending on the market, there is a good chance your offer will go up against other offers for the same home.

There's no reason to wait in getting your offer in as fast as possible to have the best chance at being the only one they're looking at.

When a seller receives an offer from a buyer they have three options in what they can do:

1. They can accept the offer

They can take your offer exactly the way that it has been presented and they can execute the contract.

2. They can do nothing

The seller can receive your offer and they can never respond or even acknowledge that they received your offer.

There's no legal requirement for them to respond to your offer.

Now obviously in most cases, the seller will respond, but understand it's not a requirement.

3. They can counter your offer

Most common is a seller to counter or accept your offer.

If they do counter, it could be based on price or on other pieces of the contract, such as the earnest money, the title company, the closing day, the inspection period and things like that.

So again, it's really important that when you find a house that you're interested in and you want to buy it, that you move quickly to purchase that home.

5. Most Buyers' Agents Represent You For Free

We'll often get the question - how is it possible that home buyer agents can represent a buyer and not get paid?

Well, they do get paid.

Buyer's agents are paid by the selling agent.

When a person lists their home for sale, they sign a listing agreement with that agent.

The listing agreement will cover things like what is the listing price, how long are they going to work together and also what the commission is.

So, let's say for example, the seller agrees to pay 6% commission. That listing broker gets to decide how to split the commission. They could keep 3% and offer 3% to the agent who represents the buyer.

The buyer's agent is being taken care of by the commission that the seller is paying.

6. Get Pre-Approved For A Home Loan Before You Start House Hunting

It's really important before you go look for a house that you know what you are qualified for.

One of the worst feelings is to go and find the home of your dreams put in an offer that's accepted by the seller, only to find out a few weeks later that you don't qualify for that amount of house and that you'll need to go find a smaller home, this is why you should always get pre-approved before you go out looking at houses.

Being pre pre-approved means that you will know exactly how much home you qualify for.

You'll know what payment to expect on homes and what price range you should consider so there'll be no surprises.

You'll know that any home you're agreeing to purchase will be within your budget and within your qualifications.

7. Understand The Home Buying Process Before You Start

There are basically seven steps to buying a house you'll want to understand.

I'm going to share the process so you will always know where you are at any given time once you start.

Step 1. Get Pre-Approved

We just talked about how important it is to get pre-approved so you will know exactly how much home you're qualified for and what your payment will be on that house.

Being pre-approved will also strengthen the offers later when you go to write that contract because the seller will have confidence knowing you've already been pre-approved for the home loan.

Step 2. Find The House

Next, you're going to hire a real estate agent and they will help represent you in finding the perfect house for you.

Your Realtor has access to every home on the market and even houses that you might not be able to find on Zillow, Realtor.com or any other websites.

These are called "pocket listings" so ask your Realtor if they know of any.

Step 3. Write an Offer and Get a Contract

Once you find the house that you want to purchase, you're going to write an offer to that seller.

This is a contract, but it's only signed by you, not by the sellers yet.

On the offer, it will include the price, when you want to close, how much money you want to put up as a down payment and all the other parts of your offer will be listed on the contract.

It is called an Executed Contract once the seller accepts and signs it.

Step 4. Get a Home Inspection

You're going to hire a 3rd party independent inspector to come in and go through the house and tell you what they find out is right and wrong about the house.

Understand that it's the inspector's job to point out everything that's wrong and they will go over the house with a fine-tooth comb and point out every tiny imperfection but that does not mean the house is not worthy of you buying it.

You have to really be purposeful with what you decide is important and fixable in the future during that inspection period.

Step 5. Home Appraisal

This will be ordered from your mortgage company, and again, an independent person will come out to the house that you're purchasing and agree on what the value of that house is.

As long as the value that the appraiser gives the house is above or equal to your contract price, then your mortgage company is going to give it the thumbs up.

If for some reason the home comes in at a lower value, either you'll need to renegotiate the contract or you may need to pay the difference out-of-pocket.

Step 6. Receive Full Loan Approval

This will let you know that you've been completely approved and you're ready to go to closing.

Everything has been done in terms of researching your credit, income, and background. The mortgage company feel confident to provide you with a home loan.

This is also the time where the documents for your home loan and all the papers that you're going to have to sign are going to be drawn up and those are going to be sent to the closing company.

Step 7. Attend Closing & Become The Owner

Now it's time to attend closing, sign all the paperwork and you will officially become the new homeowner.

Closing is when you will provide your down payment, any other funds that you are paying and any other minor fees that come up along with purchasing a home.

Now you know the 7 steps to become a homeowner.

8. Keep An Open Mind

When we say keep an open mind, what we want you to do is to know what's realistic for your budget.

If you have a $100,000 budget, that's going to purchase a different kind of home than a $300,000 budget and that budget will purchase a different home than a $500,000 budget.

Neither one of those is right or wrong, but you have to understand what's realistic for your price range.

One of the exercises that can be helpful is to-do a needs versus wants sheet side-by-side.

Take a piece of paper and make one column for needs and one column for wants.

List out things like the bedrooms and bathrooms and different features and layouts and neighborhoods and all these things that you feel are important about the house that you're going to go shopping for.

Keep in mind what's a need versus a want, right?

A need may be that you need four bedrooms but you want to have a three car garage. You have to decide which column each item fits in.

Also, there's a thing that we call the HGTV effect.

These shows about buying houses on HGTV have made some buyers not fully understand the actual process.

Any time you have questions or you want to talk about if the homes are not meeting your criteria, have that conversation with your real estate agent.

9. Choose An Agent You Like

There is a lot of trust involved when you are purchasing a home.

You should choose an agent that you enjoy working with.

You're going to spend a lot of time together, so pick somebody that you enjoy their company.

You want to pick somebody that you feel is going to look out for your best interest.

Find someone you really feel is going to represent you well.

Don't always use the first agent you come across unless you feel a connection with them.

Take some time and ask for referrals.

You can even ask your Loan Officer for some referrals since they will know the best agents.

Find a Realtor you really vibe with and that you get along with and you feel like you want to work with in this home buying process.

10. It's Important To Understand The Point Of A Home Inspection

Your home inspector is going to be an independent person who probably has never been in the house before.

They are going to have a checklist and it's going to take them several hours to complete this process.

The home inspector at the end might even invite you to the house so that they can go over what they have found.

They also provide a written report.

Keep in mind they will tell you every tiny issue that exists in that home.

While you're going-over that report, it's important to know what's important and what's not.

What is a Deal Breaker and what's not a Deal Breaker, right?

What can you ask the sellers to repair and what could you repair yourself after you move in?

One suggestion is never to ask the seller to repair every item on the inspection checklist. You want to show that you are reasonable and you're not going to ask them to repair the small things that aren't that important that you could easily do yourself when you move in.

11. Keep Your Money Wherever It's At

If you have money in the mattress, you want to get that money in the bank 6 months ahead of when you want to purchase a home.

There's a thing called seasoning and you're going to have to season that money if you want to use it for a down payment or anything that has to do with purchasing a home.

If the money is not seasoned the mortgage company will definitely ask you to prove where it came from.

They do not want to see any large deposits into your account without being easily trackable.

This of course doesn't include your normal paychecks, child support or any other money you receive on a monthly basis. But more so, large deposits that are harder to explain.

You should also know that the mortgage company will probably look at your bank accounts in the beginning of the transaction but there's also a chance that they could look again right before closing.

So, don't try to be sneaky and add $10,000 or whatever amount into your checking account right before closing.

You could lose the loan approval if they go back and look at your accounts again and see something like that.

12. Start Online But In The End Trust A Person

Everybody starts the home buying process online.

They look for homes online, they research different mortgage programs; it's a normal thing in today's age.

One thing to know is online information can be outdated or even incorrect.

There's no requirement or oversight on websites and the information that exists online.

Whatever you find online, in the end, you want to find a local professional to help you understand that information and how it pertains to you exactly.

In terms of finding a home, the same thing is true.

Start online with your home search but in the end you want to find a Realtor that you trust and work with them.

A local Realtor is also going to know about homes not available online.

Sometimes, these are referred to as "Pocket Listings" because only a few people know they exist.

Realtors will also have relationships with other agents and this can help you find homes that may not be available online.

It may also help you get the contract if you get into multiple offer situations, so it's important to start your search online but in the end trust local professionals.

13. Visit The Neighborhood Where You're Purchasing A Home In The Daytime And At Night

You want to go to your house and see how it is normally during the day.

Check thinks like what cars are around, how busy the neighborhood is and what's occurring during a normal work day.

If it's possible go back around 7 p.m. to see how it is in the evenings.

What is it like when everybody is home from work and school?

What are the neighborhood demographics?

Who do you see in the neighborhood?

Are there kids playing?

Are there people walking in the neighborhood or out enjoying the neighborhood?

What is it like in the evening time?

It's also a great idea to go to the property on the weekend to see what it's like.

What are people doing in that area?

You will get a real feel for the neighborhood by visiting a property during the daytime on a weekday, during the evening on a weekday and on a weekend.

It can sometimes be deceiving only visiting during a weekday when everyone is gone.

14. Write A Love Letter

Alright, we're not talking about writing a letter to a prisoner or to an old high school sweetheart.

In this case, we're talking about writing a letter to the seller of the home you want to purchase, telling them what you love most about the house.

This letter should be no more than one piece of paper long telling them how you vision your family living in the house.

You want to share things like what excites you about the neighborhood and why you want this transaction to move forward.

This is a great thing to include with an offer especially when you are getting into multiple offer scenarios.

15. Auctions & Bank Sales Can Be Deceiving

Oftentimes online, you will see people marketing things like pre-foreclosures or short sales or foreclosures.

On the surface they can seem like a great deal.

When you really dig in, one of the main differences is these properties are rarely move-in-ready.

Most first-time buyers, especially who have never gone through this process, forget to calculate the cost to rehab the property to make it liveable.

So when you're looking for a home and you see these fixer upper specials, keep in mind what else would be required in order to make the foreclosure your family home.

16. When Should I Talk With A Loan Officer?

You should talk to a loan officer as soon as possible.

The thing I have found when I'm talking with any potential home buyer is the first question they ask is, "Who should I talk to and how hard is it to get qualified?".

So, I feel you need to do it as soon as possible because you want to really know exactly what you qualify for.

You want to know if there's going to be any hiccups along the way.

Anything you can do to start that process and talk with your loan officer as quickly as possible will be helpful so you're not going out there wasting your time.

You don't want to be disappointed if you find a home you love but can't qualify for it. Getting pre-approved will prevent that.

17. What Credit Score Do I Need To Get A Mortgage?

The average credit score right now is a 620.

Somewhere between 620-640 is preferable with the scores today.

That doesn't mean people with a score lower than 620 are out of luck.

We have a 6 month guaranteed approval program through our credit repair partner. (Ask me for details)

Obviously, the higher the score the better. But, as we have seen in the past, there are some people that unfortunately have had some hiccups.

Everybody has had a little bit of credit dings in the past.

We prefer to get you up in the 620-640 range to get a mortgage.

There are some benefits to having a higher credit score such as having to bring a lower down payment.

The lower the score the possibility of you bringing more to the closing table might be a factor as well as the interest rate depending on what the overall credit is.

So, the higher the credit score obviously the better.

It will give you a little bit possibly better interest rates and lower down payments; that kind of thing.

18. What Will You Look At When I Apply For A Mortgage?

First thing we take a look at when you're applying for a mortgage is actually the credit score. We want to see exactly where you stand credit wise.

Then we want to look at your debt load. We'll see how much debt you're paying compared to your income.

This is called "Debt to Income Ratio" when you're getting a mortgage.

We also look to see if you have any collections.

A lot of times there are some unpaid collections or something on a credit report that people don't realize that they've had.

Maybe they had some old collection that was supposed to be paid off or an old medical bill.

There's a lot of stuff that's on there that people don't realize.

So, it's always good for us to take a look when you're applying to make sure there's no judgments against you.

These things have to be paid off before you actually go and close the loan. You either can pay them off or you can have a payment plan.

We want to make sure that you're back on track to get those things taken care of.

We also look to see if you've had a bankruptcy in the last 7-10 years.

That's going to have a determining factor on what's going on when you're applying for the mortgage.

So, all those factors are what we really look at when you apply for a mortgage.

19. What Does It Mean To Get Pre-Approved For A Home Loan?

It means you have a Loan Officer who pulled your credit, looked at your financial documents, looked everything over and they have determined you meet the guidelines.

So, getting pre-approved is the first step for you to feel comfortable buying a home.

We just talked about what we look at when applying for the mortgage, and once you have given us that information we can start doing our due diligence.

We want to match your application with your financial documents.

Everything on your application gets verified and considered to see if it meets the guidelines that are out there and that's when you get your final approval and then go to closing.

Pre-approved means we've actually gone in and looked at your financial documents and made sure that it's matching.

So, we want to make sure that it's verified and that we pre-approve you with those financial documents so we can make sure that what you're telling us is accurate.

20. What Is The Minimum Downpayment To Get A Mortgage?

Well, there are quite a few programs out there.

It's pretty cut and dry with the minimum down payments to get mortgages these days.

There are zero down options with the VA loan and USDA program.

You've also got 3.5% down options with the FHA program.

Conventional loans have options with as low as 3% down.

Those are the three most common down payment options for home loans.

21. How Much Cash Do I Need To Buy A Home?

Well, that depends on exactly what program you're applying and approved for.

Some of the fees most buyers pay at closing include:

- Home appraisal
- Home inspections
- Title closing fees
- Pre-paid taxes or insurance
- Third party fees

You will receive a closing cost estimate when you apply for a home loan showing you all the costs with the mortgage company.

22. Should I Pay Discount Points?

When the rates are very low as they have been over the last 7-8 years; it doesn't make sense to in most cases.

Many people think that if you want to buy discount or pay discount points to buy down the rate that's going to make a big difference.

You have got to look at the long term, just because you're paying discount points doesn't necessarily mean you're saving money.

You have to figure out how long you will be living in the home, and how much 'savings' you can get from paying discount points.

I tell my clients not to pay discount points and I show them the difference between the return on their money vs how long it's going to take to recoup that money when they pay the point.

We need to see exactly what they're going to get in return if they reduce the rate because of the discount point.

23. Is There A Point Where The Interest Rate Goes High Enough That It Is Worth Paying Discount Points?

Yes, at times, but everybody's got a different circumstance so that's why it's important to run a cost savings analysis to see if it makes sense to pay discount points.

It's important to have an understanding of what you're trying to accomplish, then we can look at deciding if it makes sense to pay those discount points to get that lower interest rate.

There are alot of factors involved that should impact your decision on whether or not to pay discount points.

If it's costing you $5,000 per point on a $400,000 loan; that's a lot of money.

It is smart to do the math and determine if the offset interest you will save by paying the points up front will be worth it in the long term based on your total out of pocket expenses at closing and the length of time you plan to own the home.

24. What Is The Difference Between A Fixed-Rate Mortgage And ARM Loan?

A fixed rate mortgage stays the same for the length of the loan. Nothing changes. So, if you have it for the full term of 10, 20, 30 years it stay fixed, nothing changes on that rate.

The only thing that might change is your estimates for your tax of insurance.

Now for an ARM or Adjustable Rate Mortgage, that can adjust after the initial fixed period.

Depending on what ARM program it might go up or down depending on what the market is doing.

Each type of mortgage has its own benefits but it is very important that you speak with your lender and look at each type of loan to see what best fits for your unique situation.

25. What Will My Mortgage Payment Include?

Principal, interest, tax and insurance.

We often abbreviate this as PITI.

Principal - The amount of the loan that you borrowed.

Interest- The charge that the bank or institution charges for lending you the principle.

Tax- The taxes charged by the local and state governments may be included here.

Insurance- The homeowners insurance (some people call it hazard insurance) this is to cover the home and insure that any problems or damages are able to be covered.

26. Can Someone Give Me Money For My Down Payment?

Yes, they absolutely can.

Often what we see is people's parents that are giving down payment to their kids.

You just have to make sure you're documenting it.

The documentation is key to ensuring that we understand exactly what those funds are for and that they are to be assigned to the down payment of the home.

27. Why Should I Buy A Home Instead Of Rent?

Buying a home is an asset that potentially will appreciate in value.

You buy a home at $200,000 and hopefully the value goes up as you see the market change and the growth in the area.

Having a home of your own is a financial investment. It's something you're investing in as you pay down.

It's a home and an investment that can increase in value as you own it.

There are also tax breaks involved so you're able to write certain things off when you are purchasing a home.

Somebody has even purchased the home or apartment you live in. You are paying down the balance on their investments and giving them a residual income.

So there's a big difference compared to renting.

You can't really write anything off when you rent. If there's stuff that you've bought to fix up the house you're renting, you can't write that kind of stuff off on taxes.

So there's a lot of quirks and benefits to owning instead of renting.

28. How Do I Know How Much House I Can Afford?

That's when we need to talk.

That's why you need to talk to a loan officer as soon as possible when you are considering becoming a homeowner.

You have to have a solid idea of your income and debts to understand how much you may qualify for on a mortgage.

Speaking with a loan officer sooner rather than later will help you understand where you are currently, and what will be possible in your local housing market.

Generally you want to have a good understanding of your financial situation before you start looking for a home.

So, we will calculate everything and figure out exactly what you qualify for. We will get your proof and then get you out there looking for the perfect house for you.

With all those steps in place we can be confident that you will be able to purchase it.

29. How Long Does It Take To Buy A House?

Usually it takes 30 to 45 days from the time you find the home until you close.

There could be some some circumstances that come up that might delay that process but that is a general timeline that most loans are closing in at the moment.

For example, if you purchase a short sale home it might take 3 months to get bank approval and go to closing.

30. What Can I Do If My Credit Is Messed Up?

That's a great question that I get all the time about credit. I wouldn't say everybody, but the majority of people I have financed or help buy a home over the past 12-15 years have had some kind of credit hiccup along the way.

We have a team of people to help you look at your credit score and get it where it needs to be.

It's important to look at an overall picture of your credit.

There may be things on your report that you don't realize are there.

There could also be items you had paid off and they were never removed from the report.

There are also situations like when there is a Senior and a Junior. Their credit can get mixed together.

We have a team of experts who are able to look that over and be able to get you to where you need to be to get qualified into that 620 - 640 range that we talked about earlier.

31. What Is Earnest Money?

Earnest money is the money you put in an escrow to show the seller you are serious about the offer.

Often, sellers don't want to accept just anybody's offer. So, an earnest money deposit is given to show good faith that the potential buyer is serious about purchasing the home.

32. Is There A Loan Program Available To Fix Up A House If The House Needs Repairs?

Absolutely. This is a big one throughout the country.

There's a lot of folks looking to find homes and the ones they find need repairs. The houses might have storm damage, be outdated or simply been neglected.

This is what a 203K loan is for.

203K loan is one of the ways you can buy a home and borrow money to fix it up the way you want without coming out of pocket.

Ask your Loan Officer if the home you want to purchase can qualify for the 203K program.

33. What Is A Home Appraisal?

A home appraisal is a value given to your home by a certified appraiser.

It's a 3rd party that goes out and appraises the house to give an actual true assessment of what the house is worth.

Around 2008, there was a big issue that a lot of people were inflating value. So, nowadays we take home appraisals very serious.

The appraiser will go out to other homes selling in the area and compare the subject property to them in order to give you a true value of what the home is worth. This is required for a purchase or a refinance.

34. Is There A Difference Between Buying A Home To Live In And Buying An Investment Property?

Absolutely. There's a big difference especially in the qualifying process.

You can get up to 100% financing when you are actually looking for a primary residence.

It's more secure that you are purchasing a home and living in it than getting a investment property.

You may get better interest rate and higher loan-to-value so you don't have to bring so much money at the closing.

Now when you're buying an investment property obviously it's in the name itself, it's an investment, and those require a little bit more money down.

Generally, investment homes requires about 20% down.

That applies for people that are looking to make an investment like we talked about besides their primary residence.

The biggest difference is interest rates and bringing more down payment to closing.

35. Four Questions To Ask When Buying a Flip

You've seen the pretty pictures online. The beautiful furniture, the open floor plan, quartz, stainless steel appliances, it's all new!

A home is considered 'flipped' when an investor buys a home in need of repairs, strips it down and installs a brand new interior.

Sometimes they even install new landscaping and other outdoor features.

First time buyers especially love these 'flipped' homes.

Sure, it looks fantastic and you are falling in love, but what's underneath the new facade?

Here's four questions you should ask before closing on this beauty.

What is the home's history?

Everything is public record now, so ask your Realtor for the transaction history. Why? This will show when the investor bought the home and how much they paid for it.

It will also show the square footage, bedroom and bath count.

An investor might take a patio and create a bedroom or add a shower or even a full bathroom.

As the buyer, you want to know if there's been any plumbing or electrical moved around or added.

Are there any improvements?

Ask the seller for a list of improvements and request them to document it. You want to know where those appliances came from!

This will help you during the inspection period. Especially pay attention to any electrical and plumbing that's been moved, altered or added.

Can you use your inspector?

A licensed property inspector is always a good idea. Make sure you walk around the property with him/her so they can point out anything that may need further inspection.

I would always get a lateral sewer inspection and have a licensed electrician check the panels. Lots of flippers add more electrical outlets, microwaves and other appliances without upgrading the panel. This is a possible fire hazard and will be expensive to upgrade later.

Where are the permits?

Lots of remodeled homes may have additions without permits. It is not 100% necessary for permits, but any additions should be done in a workmanship like manner.

If not, the lender may have issues when the appraisal is done. Ask the seller for the name and license number of the contractor that did the work.

If you have issues later, you have recourse against the contractor. It's a red flag if the work is not done by a contractor.

Overall, a remodeled home can be a great purchase!

Everything is done, you move right in and enjoy your new home! Just make sure everything about your new home before you close!

36. Condos Are An Affordable Path To Homeownership

Condominiums and townhomes are a great way to enter the homeownership market.

They are typically more affordable in both sales price and monthly costs.

The right complex will appreciate as much as a single family neighborhood. With recent finance changes, condominiums are easier to finance too.

Most buyers who cannot afford a single family home will say "I'll continue to rent, I don't want to pay HOA dues, they are a waste of money!".

I then ask, "Do you know what the HOA fee covers?".

Compared to the cost and maintenance of a single family home, HOA's can be a bargain!

Let's look at how this saves you money –

	Single Family Home	Condo/HOA
Water Bill	$100	$50
Gardener	$50	$0
Trash/Sewer	$50	$0
Insurance	$100	$50
Maintenance	$75	$0
Total	$475	$100
Pool	$250	$0
Total	$725	$100
HOA	$0	$350

*Costs can vary. These costs are an estimate from a typical Southern California home.

In this example, a $350 HOA fee covers $725 in costs/expenses if you have a pool.

Condominiums and townhomes are an excellent way to start investing in real estate.

You're in control of the interior and the exterior is maintained by the HOA.

Many buyers purchase a single family home and become overwhelmed with the upkeep and maintenance. Buying a home with an HOA also frees up your time.

While other homeowners are browsing the aisles of Home Depot looking for a replacement sprinkler head, you're enjoying your sparkling pool!

Owning a condo compared to renting?

There is no comparison!

With ownership you gain appreciation, equity, tax advantages and the peace of mind you can live there as long as you want.

It's truly the only way to control your long term housing expense.

37. What Are Contingencies?

The current purchase contract in California is 12 pages, there is a lot of information in there!

There are basically 3 contingencies you need to really pay attention to.

If you miss one, you are out of contract, and technically, the seller can cancel your contract and sell your home to someone else.

An experienced agent and lender will make sure you stay on schedule.

The first contingency is the **property inspection**.

The seller usually gives you between 5-15 days to order inspections and satisfy yourself as to the condition of the property.

This is the time you verify the roof doesn't leak, the sewers drain, the electrical systems are adequate and further research any red flags that these inspections discover.

Your agent will go back to the seller accepting the property as is or asking for repairs or further negotiations.

The second contingency is the **appraisal**.

Your lender will order the appraisal day 1 and the lender usually has 17 days or sooner to get the appraisal back to you. You review the appraisal, verify it came in at the sales price and requires no repairs.

The third and biggest contingency is the **loan contingency**.

When you release this contingency, this means your loan is approved and there is no reason why you cannot buy your new home.

This is where your lender needs to be positive your loan is approved and there is nothing that will cause the loan to be denied.

In this very competitive seller's market, contingencies are a great way to make your offer better than others, without paying a higher price.

Is it very easy to shorten timelines?

Shorter timelines are valuable to a seller and increases the odds of your offer being accepted.

Is it risky? Not, if done right.

An experienced agent and lender team will ensure you will not risk losing your deposit if timelines aren't met.

The appraisal gets ordered right away, sometimes on a rush.

The inspections need to be done within a few days.

We sometimes don't even write in a loan contingency, making the buyer equal to a cash buyer.

How do we do that? We fully underwrite and pre-approve the buyer BEFORE the offer is accepted.

38. Explore Your Down Payment Options

When buying a home, you basically need two piles of money.

One is for the down payment and the other is for closing costs.

Generally, closing costs are 2% of the sales price and your down payment will vary, depending on the loan type.

If you're using VA home loan benefits, you will not need a down payment, otherwise, consider these options.

401K Loan –

If you have a 401K, TSP or other retirement account, you should ask the plan administrator if you can take out a loan. Most plans allow you to borrower 50% of the balance and can usually set the interest rate and payment.

It is not a taxable event because it's not a withdrawal, you borrower the money from yourself. The lender will not count the payment against you and lower your approval amount.

IRA's do not usually allow for a loan and can only be a withdrawal.

Down Payment Grants –

Grants are available through cities, counties and states. A grant does not show up on your property and does not have to be repaid.

Most grants can cover the down payment and closing costs. There is usually a higher cost and rate, but it can be a great way to buy a home if you don't have the funds yourself.

Lender Credits –

Technically, you cannot use lender credits for a down payment. You can, however, use the credits for closing costs, saving your cash for the down payment.

If you take a credit, your lender will charge you a higher rate. You will need to look at all interest rate options to see if the higher rate is worth the extra cash at closing.

Gift Funds –

You can buy a home with zero money out of pocket if you find a nice relative to give you the cash. It's OK if you intend to occupy your new home.

The best way to utilize gift funds is to allow the donor to leave the funds in their own bank account.

The lender will simply ask for a copy of the donor's bank statement and a letter stating this money does not have to be repaid.

Borrow From an Asset –

You can borrow money on an asset if you can afford another payment in your debt ratio.

Many buyers can refinance their car if it's owned free and clear. This is an excellent way to get cash for your home purchase.

There have been recent changes in lending allowing for lower down payments, so make sure you speak with an experienced loan officer who can create a financing package that helps you meet your real estate goals.

39. Let's Talk About Sewers

It's a fact, every home must have a sewer drain.

There's basically two types. A public sewer takes all the waste water from your home into the main sewer pipes under the street.

If you live in a rural area where no public sewer is available, you will have a septic tank. This is a giant tank buried in your yard where the wastewater goes and must be pumped out occasionally.

Today we're talking about public sewers which is most common.

When purchasing a home, a lateral sewer inspection is highly recommended. During the inspection phase of your purchase, you can contract a licensed plumber to send a camera down through the main drain.
The camera will show, through a video, exactly what is clear or blocked all the way to the main sewer line in the street.

This can be a particularly big problem when buying an investor remodeled home, or a flip.

Flippers are known for cutting corners.

When a flipper demolishes a home, they do not cover the hole where the toilet goes, and all the construction debris can clog up the pipes. They then set a new toilet and never verify the drains are clear.

A normal property inspection does not discover this problem.

Once the unsuspecting buyer moves in and starts using all the plumbing, the construction debris will catch somewhere in the plumbing and causes sewage back ups anywhere there is a drain.

This is not pleasant!

Another main reason for backups are tree roots.

When the inspection camera goes through the line, you will be able to see all the dirt, cracks and roots that can block the main line. Since it's lateral, it does not really drain downhill and can easily clog with debris. This is the time you would show the video to the seller and request repairs or renegotiate a change satisfactory to both parties.

Don't find yourself on the wrong end of a clogged drain, get an inspection.

40. Attention Military - Top 5 Reasons You Want To Use Your VA Loan Benefit

If you've served our country by being in the military, you deserve this awesome benefit!

It is the best loan out there.

VA loans offer no down payment, lower rates, no mortgage insurance and generous underwriting guidelines.

Let's look at the top 5 reasons you should use your VA home loan benefit.

No Down Payment –

The national loan amount is now $453,100.

This means anywhere in the country, you can buy a home using VA financing with zero money down.

In high cost counties, mostly metropolitan areas, the max loan amount can be higher.

No PMI –

Unless you bring in 20% cash down payment, your lender will require you to buy Private Mortgage Insurance to cover them in case of a foreclosure.

Not with VA!

VA loan program is paid for with a funding fee, a one time cost added to the loan. If you have at least a 10% service related disability, this fee will be waived.

This saves the average home buyer $300-500 a month on the payment.

Generous Credit Guidelines –

VA loans are the only home loans that allow you to buy a home 2 years after a major derogatory event like bankruptcy, foreclosure and short sale.

You are also not penalized as heavily for having low credit scores. A 620 FICO score can still get you a good rate. Other loan programs require a minimum 680 to be competitive.

Qualify For a Higher Loan Amount –

Most lenders use a debt ratio to determine your ability to repay a mortgage. Not the VA!

VA loans use a residual income model. This benefits most military buyers and helps them qualify for substantially more than with other programs.

Better Interest Rates –

VA loans usually carry a lower interest rate than other programs.

Conventional loans want you to have a 720 minimum score or you will pay a substantially higher rate.

Some lenders claim they can use a 580 score, but it's really expensive!

You are better off taking a few months and improving your credit score before buying. Most VA lenders use a 620 score to get a good rate and 680+ to get an even better rate.

VA loans can be used more than once. Sometimes even before the original loan is paid off.

Your best bet is to talk to an experienced VA lender who can share their knowledge and direct you to an experienced agent.

The teamwork of a good agent/lender will ensure your offer gets accepted, your timelines met and have you moving into your home on time.

41. 15 Year Mortgage vs 30 Year Mortgage

Many times throughout the week I get asked, "What is the difference between a 15-year mortgage and a 30-year mortgage"?

I usually try and lighten up the mood a little and respond with a quick, "About 15 years or 180 monthly payments!"

Really what my borrower is trying to determine is, does it make more financial sense to sign closing papers on a 15-year mortgage or a 30-year mortgage?

So, the question I ask is, "What are you trying to accomplish by getting a 15-year loan verses a 30-year loan"?

Most of the time the answer to this question is that they just want to pay the loan off quicker than 30 years.

I am 100% fine with either loan, the borrower needs to evaluate a few key pieces to buying this home to make sure they make the right choice.

A quick Google search of a few calculators can easily answer if this makes financial sense. The first Google search I run is a mortgage calculator. For our example today, we are going to use some simplistic figures.

We will use a loan amount of $250,000 with a 4% interest rate for a 30-year note and a 3.75% interest rate for a 15-year note.

This is just an example and not a guarantee that either of these interest rates are attainable at the time of reading this book.

If we take the $250,000 loan amount with these interest rates we will quickly determine that the principal and interest payment for the 30-year note is $1194, and the payment for the 15-year note is $1818, a monthly difference of $624.

The second piece we need Google to help us with is an investment calculator. I am not guaranteeing any rate on return from an investment.

Google quickly found me an investment calculator and I entered in our $624 monthly difference for 15 years, the time difference between the 30-year note and the 15-year note.

I used an average interest rate of 6%. After 15 years of making this investment at this rate of return I found out I would have $175,785.91 in my investment account.

The final Google search led me to my amortization schedule.

Guess what it showed me?

After 15 years of paying my minimum monthly payment my balance is $161,357. I could write a check, from that investment account, for the entire amount and still have over $14,000 left over.

The financially disciplined borrower can take the difference and invest it into a non-qualified, diversified, mutual fund account with a good financial coach and have access to the money if and when you need it.

Signing the 30-year note will allow you to build up some additional wealth and should something happen, you now have access to the funds needed to do unforeseen repairs.

In the event you already have a sizeable non-qualified account to pull from maybe the 15-year mortgage is the best way to go.

42. More Money Down?

A couple times a month I will get asked questions about putting more money down on a home instead of the minimum requirement.

Usually this is a situation where a borrower has either saved up money specifically because someone told them they must put 20% down.

Sometimes this question comes up because someone wants to close out an old retirement account and utilize that money for a down payment.

I like to utilize math and financial wisdom to see how best to advise a borrower.

Let's pretend that you have saved up $50,000 for your down payment, because you thought you needed that much.

That would provide for you a $250,000 sales price on your home ($50,000 = 20% of $250,000).

Using a quick Google search to develop a base I started with a $200,000 loan amount with a 4% interest rate and a 30-year mortgage.

That quickly shows us that a monthly payment for principal and interest would be $955.

The next calculation I used was on a $241,250 loan amount, using a FHA 3.5% minimum down payment.

Our payment is now $197 more per month.

The answer to whether the borrower should invest the extra money depends on their whole financial picture.

If you took that same $41,250 and put it in a shoebox under your bed, each month you could go grab the extra $197 to pay your mortgage payment and you would have money in that shoe box for over 209 months, that's over 17 years!

A quick Google search for an investment calculator shows us that averaging 3% rate of return on that $41,250 would give us $68,179.96 after those same 17 years and if we left it alone for the full 30 years that we pay on our mortgage we would have over $100,000!

So, a good rule of thumb is to realize that on average you will only save about $5 per month for every $1000 that you put down on the mortgage.

Is it worth saving $5 per month?

The answer is completely up to you, the borrower.

I have had many people put the extra money down because they had saved the money for this specific purpose and they know their monthly budget will allow the payment at the lower amount.

They usually fear that if they choose to keep the money they will spend it on something else and their monthly budget will be out of tune.

I have also had many families decide to use that money to start an investment account with a local financial advisor and treat the purchase of their home like an investment tool.

43. Do You Like To Gamble?

Throughout each month I am probably asked a million times, "Well what is the interest rate?"

Here is the amusing piece to that question, if I were to ask someone what the interest rate on their home is currently, 80% have no idea!

This is only a question that matters when financing the home.

So naturally a follow up question usually is, "What would you like it to be?"

Our local market is pretty competitive and most mortgage bankers in this area have virtually the same rates, so shopping for an interest rate usually doesn't make up for the time spent shopping.

After all, isn't the purpose of a lower rate to be a lower monthly payment?

Here is where I let, you, the borrower make a choice.

Do you like to gamble?

We can look at rates all the way down to the lower 3% range.

That only means if you want that rate, you better be willing to pay for it!

So what does gambling have to do with anything?

Well if you pay for a lower interest rate we need to determine when you will make up that investment.

Let's define a term really quick.

A "discount point" is 1% of the loan amount.

So, 2 points would be 2%. When buying down a interest rate you use discount points. A 3.75% rate could cost you 1.35 discount points, or 1.35% of the loan amount.

For the next few minutes we need to determine a scenario.

We found a perfect home for $235,000. We will utilize a 3.5% down payment program to give us a loan amount of $226,775 ($235,000 – 3.5% ($8,225) = $226,775)

A quick jump to a Google calculator will show you that the difference between a 4.25% and 4.125% is between $16 and $17 per month.

Let's make an assumption that for every 1/8 of an interest rate (.125%) the fee is half of a point or .5%.

So for our scenario a 4.25% interest rate would cost you $0 in discount points, but for a 4.125% (an 1/8 difference) it would cost you half a point, or $1133.87.

Are you with me so far?

Now we need to determine how many months of saving our $16-$17 per month it will take to recover the initial cost.

So for our mathematicians out there, we take the difference in payment from the original payment to the new payment ($1116-$1099 = $17).

The we divide that into the cost of the buy down to determine months to make up payment ($1133.88 / $17 = 66.70).

So, for us to invest $1133.88 up front it would take us 66.70 months or just over 5.5 years.

So, do you like to gamble? Will you be in this same house for more than 5.5 years?

Here is a quick table of what the fee would be to "buy down" the interest rate and the number of months it would take to recover that fee based on our example:

This is not a guarantee of what the discount fees cost, this is just an example.

Loan Amount		$226,775		
rate	price	cost	payment	month to make up payment
4.250%	0	$ -	$1,116	0.00
4.125%	0.5%	$1,133.88	$1,099	66.70
4.000%	1%	$2,267.75	$1,083	68.72
3.875%	1.5%	$3,401.63	$1,066	68.03

3.750%	2%	$4,535.50	$1,050	68.72
3.625%	2.5%	$5,669.38	$1,034	69.14
3.500%	3%	$6,803.25	$1,018	69.42

44. How Can I Best Be Prepared To Get A Home Loan

On the back of my business card I share the 10 commandments of Home Buying. This is a very resourceful tool to anyone looking to get ready to buy a home.

Here they are:

1. Thou shalt not change jobs, become self-employed or quit your job

2. Thou shalt not buy a car, truck or van (or you may be living in it!)

3. Thou shalt no use credit cards excessively or let current accounts fall behind

4. Thou shalt not spend money you have set aside for closing costs

5. Thou shalt not omit debts or liabilities from your loan application

6. Thou shalt not buy furniture on credit

7. Thou shalt not originate any additional inquiries on your credit

8. Thou shalt not make large deposits without checking with me first

9. Thou shalt not change bank accounts

10. Thou shalt not co-sign for a loan with anyone

I think some of these are fairly obvious why you shouldn't do them, but let's break them down just to make sure.

1. Thou shalt not change jobs, become self-employed or quit your job.

Most loan programs require a minimum of 30 days on a job, as long as you have been in that same line of employment, or education for that position before you can get a loan. The longer you have been employed in the same line of work the stronger the file. If you jump to self-employment, you need 2 years' worth of tax returns to verify income.

2. Thou shalt not buy a car, truck or van (or you may be living in it!).

Not only will this drop your credit score due to the number of auto loan inquiries, but it could also increase your payment on this liability and knock you out of being able to purchase.

3. Thou shalt no use credit cards excessively or let current accounts fall behind/

The underwriting team will always pull a soft pull credit report to insure debts, and monthly obligations have not increased.

4. Thou shalt not spend money you have set aside for closing costs.

The loan officer will turn in bank statements to show stability of savings account and proof of funds to close, if you spend that money you can rest assured that your loan will not close on time.

5. Thou shalt not omit debts or liabilities from your loan application.

This is basically lying about debts. If you omit them, when the debt is discovered the underwriting team will question why it was omitted and the loan process will start over.

6. Thou shalt not buy furniture on credit.

Just wait until you close on the house. Most of the time this is done because you get such a great deal and save 10% by purchasing today. When shopping for new furniture, just tell the sales person, "I am closing on my house in a few weeks and cannot buy today, I am just looking."

7. Thou shalt not originate any additional inquiries on your credit.

New inquiries on credit makes underwriters think there is new debt.

8. Thou shalt not make large deposits without checking with me first.

Large deposits are always suspicious. Check with your loan officer to see what the definition of large deposit is on the loan program you are using for your home purchase.

9. Thou shalt not change bank accounts.

Why would you want to change banks in the middle of the largest financial transaction of your life? If you hate your current bank that much, change after we close on your new home.

10. Thou shalt not co-sign for a loan with anyone.

Co-signing on a loan now makes you liable for that loan as well. So now we must start over with this new debt on your application.

45. Prepare Early & Seek The Advice Of A Trusted Mortgage Advisor

When buying a home, you want to make sure everything is lined up the best you possibly can.

Do not start shopping, or even, looking at homes until you have a few pieces of information lined up.

First, identify what is your maximum monthly payment, including taxes and insurance, that your budget will allow.

Knowing this number is more important than knowing how much of a house you can qualify to buy.

If your maximum monthly payment is $2,000 you will not be able to buy a $500,000 home.

Different loan programs have different guidelines on how much you can pay for your mortgage based on the amount of income you earn.

This is called your front debt to income ratio.

The goal here is to establish a price range of homes that you will feel comfortable with paying each month.

After you have determined what your monthly budget will allow in a payment, start gathering a few needed documents.

I recommend starting a file folder on your computer, or paper copy if you prefer.

Start saving items to this file so that you can quickly upload them to the loan file electronically or email them to your loan officer.

Every loan program will need 2 years' worth of tax returns with all W2's used to determine the income. Having color copies of your driver's license and social security cards are much easier to read.

We will need 30 days' worth of paycheck stubs from everyone on the loan application.

We will need the past 2 months of bank statements.

Ideally this is a checking and savings account where the money for closing is kept.

List out the last 2 years of employment with the name of the company, address and who to contact for verification.

It would be nice to have this for your past 2 years of residence history as well.

If you are applying for a VA loan, there are other documents needed like your DD-214 and Certificate of Eligibility.

If you are paying or receiving child support we will need the documents showing a current status, especially if you are using this as part of your income on the application.

Sometimes people chose to use some of the funds from their 401(k) for down payment and closing coast, if that is you then you'll need to provide those statements as well.

Finally, if you are receiving social security or disability income, we would need the documents showing the monthly amount received.

Being prepared makes your job very simple, as well as the job for you loan officer and banking team.

Sometimes it takes many months to find the perfect house.

Utilize the file folder recommendation mentioned earlier and send only what is needed at the time you sign the home purchase contract. You should also understand that delays in receiving needed documents could delay the loan process.

In conclusion, I think the biggest thing when anybody is purchasing a home is to get pre-approved first.

What most people think is that they need to talk to a Realtor first. They want to go ask the Realtor a ton of questions about the home buying process and neighborhoods and payments when they haven't even found if they can qualify for a mortgage.

I tell people, "The best thing to do before you go and get yourself all excited on the internet looking at all these homes you want to purchase, you've got to make sure that you're qualified first. Do that before you get in a Realtor's car and have them showing you homes."

So, that's why you need to go ahead and talk with your Loan Officer as quick as possible.

Find out what you qualify for, get a pre-approval letter and then you're off to the races to purchase your home.

Are You Ready To Get Started?

Reach out and let's chat...

Louis Schornstein (NMLS #5490)

888-999-1929

lschornstein@ptmcorp.net

275 Route 22 East

Springfield, NJ 07081

Equal Housing Lender

PTMCorp.net